ROUGH STUFF
FOR *HOME GUARDS AND*
MEMBERS OF H.M. FORCES

Other books by
ANDREW G. ELLIOT :—

SHOOTING TO KILL.

The Home Guard Encyclopedia
(part author and editor)

Hell ! I'm British.

Alternative to Chaos.

ROUGH STUFF

FOR HOME GUARDS AND MEMBERS OF H.M. FORCES

By
SYDNEY DUFFIELD
and
ANDREW G. ELLIOT

The Naval & Military Press Ltd

Published by

The Naval & Military Press Ltd

Unit 5 Riverside, Brambleside
Bellbrook Industrial Estate
Uckfield, East Sussex
TN22 1QQ England

Tel: +44 (0)1825 749494

www.naval-military-press.com
www.nmarchive.com

*In reprinting in facsimile from the original, any imperfections are inevitably reproduced
and the quality may fall short of modern type and cartographic standards.*

Contents.

CLOSE QUARTER WEAPON TECHNIQUE
by SYDNEY DUFFIELD.

CHAPTER I.

CHAPTER II.

CHAPTER III.

CHAPTER IV.

INTRODUCTION.

THE *Telegraph* of February 2nd, 1942, carried a brilliant feature article by their correspondent, Campbell Dixon, on his interview with the famous Sergeant York. I take the liberty of quoting a few lines : ". . . . he tried to get tough at first. He called out some order in German, and seven of his men charged me from 20 yards away with fixed bayonets. But none of 'em had much luck. I dropped the last with my automatic pistol 10ft. away. How many shots did I need? I'd sho' hate to have needed more'n seven. . . ."

Early in 1941 I wrote in *Shooting to Kill*, " A test of efficiency would occur when a position is charged. . . . The inexperienced soldier will be bewildered, because, as he would say,—if he lived to tell the tale—he had no time to aim. Any shots which he fired would be wild, and would have small chance of killing. The experienced shot, on the other hand, should have no difficulty in bagging five Nazis in a charge as short as 50 yards. Pick out your enemy and shoot him. . . ."

The *Telegraph* extract more than confirms my statement of a possibility. I quote it because I wish to stress that when indicating that something can be done, I try to understate rather than to exaggerate, although I know some who read me imagine the opposite to be the case.

7

This new book, *Rough Stuff*, has been hatched for several reasons. I thought *The Home Guard Encyclopedia* would be my last writing on this topic, but since it came out my publisher and I have received information indicating that so much remains to be done, we both feel another book worth while.

Sydney Duffield's contribution on bayonet fighting provides valuable unorthodox, but vital instruction. The bayonet fixed to the rifle is not at all the obsolete weapon many think. In truth, rightly used and at the right time, it is the most awe-inspiring weapon in the soldier's tool chest. This must not be taken to mean that either Mr. Duffield or I favour Lord Croft and his pikes, with which he can do what he likes.

Brighter training methods, special uses for shot guns and the subject of the fifth column in England are among other matters dealt with.

In spite of minor shortages of equipment, everywhere I go I find the greater fault is that the men are inexpert in using the weapons already provided. The weakness of the Home Guard is too much theory and too little practice. Too long wasted on academic explanations and insufficient time alloted to realistic training in the tough business of fighting.

War is a savage and brutal thing waged without mercy or quarter, and the main idea behind *Rough Stuff* is to help British soldiers to be mentally and physically prepared to meet a ruthless enemy on even or better terms.

A.G.E.

CLOSE QUARTER WEAPON TECHNIQUE

By SYDNEY DUFFIELD

CHAPTER I.

The Up-to-date Bayonet.

WHY BAYONETS WILL ALWAYS BE REQUIRED.
URGENT NEED FOR INSTRUCTION.

THERE will always be a bayonet as part of a soldier's equipment because, in certain conditions, no other weapon can take its place. In pitch-black nights, in thick smoke screens or in fog, when a man has almost to touch another before identification is possible, the bayonet is the tool. When ammunition is running low, it is a man's last resort, and often an excellent one. In fighting in narrow streets, in undergrowth, in trenches or in buildings, shooting might be out of the question owing to the intermingling of friends and foes.

The new short bayonet might also be used as a dagger, but since it is unlikely that this new weapon will be issued to the Home Guard for a very long time, all Home Guards *should carry either daggers or rigid knives*, in addition to bayonets and rifles. This is the practice of the Nazis and we would do well to imitate it. Instructors should emphasise these matters, because

9

many men to-day imagine that bayonets are
superfluous and neglect training in their use.

A bayonet thrust through the heart of a sentry
brings death in silence and there is no calling out
of the guard.   In searching farmyards, coal dumps
and such hiding places the bayonet is ideal for
testing purposes and enemies hiding behind coats
in cupboards have a strong dislike for its point!

The bayonet is an offensive weapon with one
serious limitation—its range is approximately five
feet.   That limitation must never be forgotten,
but cold steel must not be regarded as obsolete
simply for this reason. The Japanese, for example,
regard bayonet work of such importance that they
practice points against Chinese prisoners who have
their arms bound behind them.   On the other
hand, the Germans and the Italians have an un-
conquerable aversion to cold steel, which is very
much to the advantage of the British.

Some men seem to have been born with a rifle
in the hand, but most men have to be trained in
its use.   A small proportion may not yield to
treatment and must be given up as hopeless.   This
fact should be realised.   It is senseless to go on
month after month trying to make a bayonet
fighter out of a Home Guard who simply cannot
master the weapon.   Such men are best detailed
for other jobs, and in the event of an invasion
there will be plenty for them to do.   Those lack-
ing in bayonet sense may make excellent snipers
or runners carrying ammunition along the line.

In the preliminary discussion, before getting
down to actual instruction, it is as well to stress

the point that in this sort of fighting there are no rules whatever. Fred Perry, one of the greatest tennis players of all time, uses no orthodox strokes, but gets his results. The same tactics apply to bayonet fighters. They should be prepared to fight regardless of the Queensberry rules. A bayonet attack should include the ability to ram the opponent with the head, to skim a helmet at him, slash him, jump on him, tackle him as in a Rugger scrum or put him out of action in any possible way. If the attack be parried, use the butt; if one thrust fails, try another.

It is a brutal business, I well know. Few could fight in this way in cold blood, but blood soon heats in war. " Seeing red " is a liberal translation of the fury that should overcome a man. There is only one way to look at it: Kill or be killed.

Every instructor must urge on his men not only the need for courage and controlled anger—that is the true fighting spirit—but also for lightning moves and rapidity of thought. *If you want to live, get your blow in first.* If you want to win, follow it up again and again and never give the other man time to rally. Don't pause until the enemy is destroyed. Give him neither time nor quarter. If you can, frighten the life out of him by grimaces and feints before you take it from him. Act like a savage. Cruel it may be, but it is war. Remember that it is a survival of the quickest, not of the fittest.

The successful lover is the man who gives free rein to his love. So the successful bayonet fighter is he who lets his hate dominate him and holds back nothing. There must be no reluctance, no squeamishness, only absolute confidence, absolute determination to go in Hell for leather—*and win.*

Some units do not go in for bayonet practice, or only in a very superficial way. If you are attached to one of these, do your own practising. Get a friend to oppose you and both of you try out every trick until you are matched so evenly that not a Hun that is born would have a chance if he came up against either of you. The scabbard must, of course, be kept on and great care taken to avoid hurting each other.

Remember, bayonet work is not come by in a day. Muscles and nerves unaccustomed to the technique will never stand the strain against experienced enemies. The reasons for practice and more practice with the bayonet are identical with those for continual shooting practice brought out in *Shooting to Kill.**

Bayonet training need not be dull routine. The secret is to make it exciting and interesting from start to finish—to work up enthusiasm, since without that the application of the theories will lack life and originality.

In succeeding pages I propose to list numerous different lessons which can be varied and adapted to suit units in different parts of the country. I have already said, and instructors must emphasise the point, that there are no hard and fast rules. Fundamental training is essential so that men may become, as it were, part and parcel of their rifles and bayonets: their weapons must be like extra

* *Shooting to Kill,* by A. G. Elliot, 1s. 6d.

limbs. When this complete familiarity has been achieved, individual styles will develop of their own accord—and, like all individual and unexpected methods, they will not be easy to tackle.

CHAPTER II.

Real Bayonet Technique.

THE Iron Rule : Remember that the range
of a bayonet is five feet. In actual warfare,
therefore, keep a bullet in the chamber, for
it is useless to charge a man at twenty-five yards
if he is about to shoot you.

Classes : These can be formed either out of
doors or under cover. The best plan is for the
teacher to put himself in the centre of a circle so
that all his pupils can see him. From one to two
dozen men are sufficient for one instructor. Before
the class begins it is imperative to see that every
rifle is examined to make certain that it is not
loaded. This can be done either by the N.C.O.
or by each man inspecting his neighbour's rifle.
The instructor's rifle must also be examined.
" Any one with ammunition?" should be asked
invariably and if this is the case, such ammunition should be deposited. In this way accidents
will be avoided.

For the purpose of practising parrying and such
movements, the order can be given, " Open ranks
for bayonet fighting," " Rear rank about turn,

odd numbers, front rank, even numbers of the rear rank, six paces forward, march," "About turn," " The whole one pace right close, march."

In this elementary training the bayonets should be fixed with their scabbards on, and, in case they fly off, it is best to tie the latter on with string. The class should be turned to the flank when demonstrating a new movement. The instructor should show the correct stances and grips and have the class imitate him. Bayonet work is very tiring and N.C.O.s should not only tell the men to " rest " frequently, but should advise them that if anyone feels unequal to the job he should fall out or take extra " rest." A lesson totalling three-quarters of an hour is enough for one day.

Lesson 1.—Bayonet Fixing : The weight of a bayonet upsets the balance of a rifle for shooting and therefore it should only be fixed at the last moment. Since this fixing may have to be done at speed, practice is essential. Instruct the men to fix their bayonets in the ordinary way a few dozen times till they are entirely familiar with the process. Then let them practise fixing in the prone position and while actually on the move. For training purposes, when fixing at the double, scabbards must be retained, since there is always a slight risk of a man falling and accordingly stabbing himself. It will be found on examination that a man has to stop running for just one second in order to slip the bayonet's spring home. But throughout this lesson let the guiding rule be speed in fixing, rather than absolute correctness of detail in method.

Lesson 2.—"On Guard": All former soldiers know this position, but it is well to run over it before going further. Step forward one easy pace with the left foot, at the same time throwing the rifle up from the "order" position and catching it with the left hand well forward, about midway between chamber and foresight. The right hand grasps it firmly in the small of the butt. In a comfortable position the rifle is slightly inclined to the left.

This position is fundamental and mastery of it essential. The right hand should grip the small of the butt tightly and should be well over—the hand being in front of the navel. The right forearm rests along the upper part of the stock, *thereby taking the bulk of the weight of the rifle*, leaving the left hand free to *guide* or *direct* the points.

The left arm should not be fully stretched, as this gives a longer reach when the points are made. The left hand hold is not as in shooting, because the thumb comes over the top of the barrel to prevent an enemy knocking the weapon out of the holder's hands.

The left knee should be slightly bent and the right foot flat on the ground, toe pointing to right front. The bayoneteer should retain an upright position, leaning neither backwards nor forwards. To test the correctness of the stance, try pivoting on the balls of the feet; if the position is right, this should be easy.

The bayonet should point either at the base of the throat of the instructor, if he is in the centre of a circle, or at a man's opposite number, if the

B

men are in rows. The eyes must be fixed on the target, that is the spot into which the bayonet would be thrust.

The position is one of alertness and readiness to attack. Practise also coming on guard with the right foot forward and while walking and charging. But just as a child must walk before it can run, so the "on guard" stance must be mastered while standing before anything else is attempted.

For resting, merely lower the butt gently—rifles should never be banged to the ground: it's bad for them—near the toe of the right foot. Repeat this training until practice makes perfect.

Faults : The supreme fault is over concentration, bred from keenness and lack of weapon familiarity. The novice on horseback is tense and " het up," while Buffalo Bill rides as easily as you and I sit on a chair. Over concentration and muscle rigidity must be broken down and an easy manner adopted. Your rifle must become your friend, as indeed it is, and there is no royal road, only practice, practice, practice.

Among other faults are: Leaning too far back, not having the thumb round barrel, butt held too high, forearm of right hand not taking weight of rifle, not being, as it should, along the top edge of the butt. Some allow the butt to hang low or bend the left arm too much to give sufficient control of the weapon. Another beginner's error is to look at the bayonet, instead of at the target. " Keep your eye on the ball " is a very sound rule.

Instructors should never shout at their men, but should tell them carefully what is wrong and show how to rectify it by example. Teaching requires both patience and personality, and if the instructor has neither, he should return to the ranks. There is no disgrace in not being a good teacher; such are born, not made.

Lesson 3.—High Port : The reason for the so-called " High Port " is to eliminate the danger of stabbing one of your own side while charging. It is also less tiring and an easy position from which to bring down the bayonet for the final assault. To attain it, the same grip is used as in " On Guard," then close the left elbow till the left wrist is in front of the left shoulder and the right arm and hand in line with the right side of the bayonet belt.

Practise high port in the open. In climbing obstacles, the left hand holds the rifle and the right is free to assist progress. In an attack, assume the " On Guard " position when about fifteen yards from the target.

Lesson 4.—Long Point : This point is made from the "On Guard" stance. For training purposes, your opponent will be well out of range, your objective being his throat. The left hand guides the bayonet, while the right hand, with the weight of the body behind it, gives punch to the thrust. Deliver the point to the full extent of the left arm, left knee bent, body well forward, right leg braced, heel of right foot slightly off the ground, but not sufficiently to lose balance. Remember to keep the butt well under the right forearm and grip tightly with the right hand, this puts power into the thrust.   Grunting as the point is made is a psychological help which puts "pep" into it.

Faults: The instructor should check for faults. The most common one is to draw the rifle back before the point is made—a bad fault, as it uncovers the body and gives a wily opponent a momentary opening.

Other common mistakes are: Eyes not on target; butt held too high or too low; left knee not sufficiently bent; right heel not raised; whole position too rigid and inflexible.

It usually takes weeks of training to make us expert.

Lesson 5.—Withdrawal from Long Point : This is naturally practised while making the Long Point.   Just as in making the Long Point, the blade is sent straight forward, so, in withdrawing, it is drawn straight back until the right hand is well behind the hip.   The left forearm should hit you across the chest from the force of the withdrawal.   The bayonet should never be twisted, either in practice or in the real thing.   The most important thing usually overlooked by the learner is *to come back on guard at once after withdrawal to be ready for the next point or the next man.*

The strong withdrawal is used in action or with dummies if the bayonet is stuck.   Slip the left hand up to the piling swivel to increase power and withdraw in the usual manner, *then back "On*

Guard!'' If the dummy is on the ground, place one foot on the "body" before withdrawing left hand up to piling swivel, and then immediately *back "On Guard."*

Lesson 6.—Short Point : Short point has a range of three feet. From "On Guard" pull rifle back to the full extent of the right arm, slipping left hand up to the piling swivel, or where it used to be if the new rifles are used—that is, just behind the bayonet handle. This shortens the reach. Deliver the point as in Long Point to the full extent of the left arm, then withdraw and back "On Guard." A low or high point is achieved by raising or lowering the butt. Always keep the eye on the target. The importance of the short point in fighting is that if the opponent should sidestep or the long point should fail, the short point is required—and quickly! It is also needed in trenches.

The long and the short point should be practised together at speed. The order can be given, "Long point, slip left hand up as you withdraw; short point, back 'On Guard.'" Practise with left foot forward and then with right foot advanced. Give rest pauses.

Lesson 7.—The Jab : This is used for very close-quarter work, perhaps at night, or if gripped by the enemy. From position of short point, slip right hand above magazine, left hand up to bayonet handle (Ross or Winchester) and lower butt almost to ground. With the new short bayonets the jab will be easier.

The rifle is now in an almost upright position close in to the body. Now bend the knees and make a quick upward thrust. Speed is everything. Aim at your opponent's chin. This thrust covers only a few inches and as the knees are well bent, the entire weight is behind it. The butt can either be between the feet or on the right side. In practising the men must be careful not to stab themselves, especially with the new short bayonet.

Practise long point, short point, jab, in sequence and back " On Guard."

Lesson 8.—The Throw Point : A fleeing enemy just out of reach can be dispatched with the throw point. The point is similar to the long point, except that the left hand is removed and the rifle sent forward by the right arm with great force and to the full extent. With the right foot forward greater reach is obtained. Practise only on hanging sacks or dummies, otherwise bayonets may be broken through the possibility of falling to the ground.

Oblique Points : When these are made, carry the left foot off in the direction of the point.

I will end this chapter on the same note as I began, stressing the need for a round in the chamber of the rifle when in a real show-down. The safety catch should be off, as in close actions there is no time for slipping it forward.

This life-saving bullet may come in very handily if you are attacked by two of the enemy at once. Shoot one and bayonet the other. You may also be enabled to help a comrade in difficulties.

Again, you can take a snap shot at an enemy
lurking in a shellhole, and break an obstruction
if the bayonet becomes stuck in a body.   The
bullet can be used to shoot down a retreating
enemy, and has other possibilities.

Above all, don't forget after a point to get back
to the ready.   In bayonet fighting, as I well know,
targets can come in fast on all sides.

CHAPTER III.

Keeping a Whole Skin.

The Psychological Factor. . . . The Parry. . . Exciting Substitute for Assault Course.

YOU fear the bayonet. So do I. But in war there are grave personal risks which must be assumed and assessed and concerning which a sense of proportion must be held. My present intention is to enable you to assess this fear as its true value, and, so far as possible, to dissipate it, since by so doing you increase by a hundred fold your chances of keeping a whole skin. The ideal point of view is to respect your enemy's bayonet and to realise that you may be killed, but at the same time to decide that you yourself will be so expert with the weapon that unless by the chances of war you meet a man who is more than your match, it is the enemy who will feel the cold steel and not yourself.

Self confidence is the foundation of *morale*. Practice in any accomplishment provides confidence and knowledge power. Your attitude, therefore, should be : " I shall not be afraid; I know the worst, but I shall do my best to frighten the daylights out of my opponent." ''' The battle that you think you cannot win is a battle lost.''

It is not your particular wish to kill this particular man, but he happens to be an enemy. For that reason and for the sake of the cause for which you are fighting, he must be destroyed in order that freedom may live. So far as you are concerned, your will to kill is only an inversion of your will to live. It is this dominant, persevering will to live, this natural, primal urge of self-preservation, which generates the urgent determination and the cool head, both of which are essential mental preparations before going into battle. It is well to understand these things, so that the mind can be clear and the resolution firm: without these two fundamentals no man can fight his best.

So far as you, an individual, are concerned, even though a retreat or rearguard action has been ordered for tactical reasons, it must be your unfailing determination not to allow the initiative to pass to your enemy. If you lose the initiative momentarily, during a fight, get it back. The odds are with you, for as a rule the German thinks more slowly than the Britisher. In a hand-to-hand fight, give the enemy no chance to think, to breathe or to turn: keep your head and attack and attack again and again: follow up every advantage and use any or every trick in your locker—tricks which I am hoping to present to you.

Why should you not be unduly afraid of the enemy's bayonet? Because you know—although he may not—*that a little tap in the right place*

will push it aside. So long as you are not afraid,
you can make use of the parry : but once your
courage fails you, it is good-bye to all that.
Therefore the greatest importance should be
attached to the practice of parrying.

*The Right and Left Parry : Keep your eyes
fixed on the opponent's bayonet, that is, on the
target. From the "On Guard," when you are within range, straighten the left arm vigorously. Don't
bend the wrist or twist the bayonet, but slant the
latter just far enough to the right or left—which-
ever parry you are practising—to deflect the
enemy's point from your body. No need to parry
widely—indeed, that is dangerous, as you uncover
your guard and an enemy who knew his job could
at once employ the butt stroke. If you have acted
rightly and you both continue to advance, your
point should *still be on him.* Care is required in
practice, even with scabbards fixed. After parrying, withdraw, back "On Guard" again. Train
also for parrying the short point. Also practise
parrying from the jab position and use the butt
for protecting the legs. It's very easy, try it.

Remember, your opponent has but slight control
of the point of his bayonet. The least tap to
either side will cause him to miss you. The top
and side of a bayonet are not sharpened, so parrying can be carried out with the bare hands. This
method ought frequently to be practised, as it in-
creases confidence and removes "bayonet phobia,"
but for training retain the scabbard. In the heat

---

* It is better to practise parries with a parry stick, as
this eliminates the risk of damaging rifles.

of battle parrying may often have to be done with the hands if the rifle is knocked away or lost.

Another idea worth remembering is to use the helmet to turn a point aside if caught unarmed. Parries should be practised until the technique becomes instinctive, for at close quarters there is no time to think.

Catching a Blow : A sudden blow at the head with a stick or rifle can be caught by raising your weapon horizontally above the head with both hands.

Bayonet Practice : When working in ranks, practise points at first in a stationary position and then while advancing. Pass the opposing man right shoulder to right shoulder at High Port, then about turn and "On Guard." All these points can be practised in this way and, providing the ranks are not too near one another. Practise in parrying can also be carried out.

Excellent experience is gained by using the practice stick. Have one man with the stick to each half dozen Home Guards. The stick is made by having a circle of wire three inches in diameter tied to one end and a pad of sack cloth to the other. The pole should be six feet in length and should be given to a good soldier, or the holder may be hurt. The ring is used to give experience in direction of points, while the padded end is used for butt strokes and kicks. The instructor holds the pole. He holds one or other end within range of a recruit, giving the command, " You," whereupon the recruit has either to make his point or use the butt as the case may be. This provides an exciting and useful form of training.

Exciting Substitute for Assault Course : Always aim at making training thrilling and surprising. Bayonet practice can be fun if a spot of imagination is used. Sacks and dummies should have circular targets sewn into them. At first they can be hung from the branch of a tree and secured to the ground, or fixed in some other manner. The instruction should explain that a penetration of about four inches, delivered with force in a vital place will create a fatal wound. The vital parts, in the order named, are throat, head, stomach, heart region : if attacking from behind, head, back of neck, lungs, heart and kidneys. The most important thing, however, is to get the thrust home with speed and force and come "On Guard" again after each point.

Later on the sacks can be placed in all sorts of unusual spots where men would be likely to hide—in cupboards and under beds for practice in house searching. Out in the open, behind trees, in ditches, in old farm carts, in slight hollows in the ground and any other convenient spot. Give the Home Guard a time limit in which to find the dummies and divide them into groups or teams. The team which finds and pierces all the targets in the shortest time becomes the winner.

CHAPTER IV.

The Hand-to-Hand Fight.

THE SLASH. . . . THE BUTT STROKE. . . . THE
DAGGER AND ITS USE. . . . KICKS, STONES
AND HELMETS. . . . KILL OR BE KILLED. . . .
LIGHTNING REACTIONS.

THE point of the bayonet is made for use. A
thrust is always better than a butt stroke,
but in the whirlwind of hand-to-hand fighting,
the fighter must know what to do if his point
is parried, or if he is surprised when his rifle
is unloaded, or in similar disadvantageous
circumstances.

Here are some butt strokes. Again there are
no rules, and the idea which works best, wins.

The Butt Stroke: From "On Guard" swing the
butt in a circular movement, bringing the toe of
the butt to the jaw or ribs or even against the
forearm of the enemy if the other positions are
"covered." Use force.

Again, the rifle can be gripped in the vertical
position and the toe of the butt brought up with
force into the opponent's crutch or stomach. He
won't like that.

In training follow the butt stroke with the slash.
This means bringing the butt back into the "On

Guard'' position, and while doing so the slash is made with force across the face or neck.

All these movements require practice, with care taken not to use force or hurt one another. In training, keep out of range.

The Answer to the Butt Stroke: Suppose, having parried the bayonet, the butt stroke is used against you. Seize the butt of your opponent's rifle with the left hand: with your right hand grasp the barrel near the enemy's left. Next, twist the rifle upwards and over his left shoulder, at the same time kneeing him hard in the crutch. He will let go and you can then finish off the job with his rifle.

The Dagger or Fixed Knife : The first rule about a dagger in war time is to carry it in an accessible place. A sheath could be improvised let into the seam on the right side of the trouser at the knee. Be sure to learn through continual practise how quickly you can draw it, and go on practising until this quick draw becomes second nature, for when life or death hangs on a split second, it is useless to fumble.

The dagger will come in usefully for many purposes apart from actual fighting, but here is one illustration of how it can be used to save your life. Suppose you are attacked in the dark by a powerful enemy who has got hold of your rifle. Surprise him by making him a gift of it, and with the speed of greased lightning make him a further present of your dagger through his throat, heart or stomach.

If by any chance you have no dagger in such a situation, let the rifle go and dive in a flying tackle—as in Rugger—for his feet. The surprise consequent on your relinquishing the rifle will make it simple to unbalance him. Violent kicks are then indicated while you make an attempt at the same time to recover your weapon.

THE FIGHT.

During training it should be impressed on recruits that the purpose of bayonet practice is to provide fundamental teaching. This ground work, having been learned and practised until it has become instinctive, when the real thing starts, confidence and intelligence will tell you what to do and when to do it.

Imagine that you have just polished off one Nazi and come back to "On Guard" when another rushes at you. As he thinks he has his bayonet through you, you sidestep and fool him. Next you approach each other, each making feints for an opening. This is done by pretending to go for the face and then alternately the body and seizing an opening or beating the opponent's weapon aside, to get your thrust home. He flings his rifle at you, but you jump aside, he then leaps towards you with his dagger, but you are in time to parry his arm with your rifle, using your butt, but he steps clear. As you do so he jams his heavy boot on to your instep. Luckily the ground is soft and you can still stand.

By now, you are both growling and grimacing at one another and behaving pretty much like savages. Remember that in this form of warfare

he is the more successful who inspires the greater
fear, and from your own point of view the noise
you make bucks you up no end in the dirty game
of hand-to-hand combat.

You rush over to prevent him from regaining
his rifle, but as you do so he grabs a stone and
hurls it at your head. You duck and his bluff
has worked, for he has seized *your* rifle and in
the struggle he forces it from you, having used
the backheel to unbalance you.

But before he has time to stab you, you have
rolled clear, leapt to your feet and skimmed your
helmet straight into his teeth. The rest should
be easy.

One could continue indefinitely with tips and
ideas. Use your orthodox methods of fighting—
the parry and long point and short point—but they
may have to be augmented for rough and tumble
methods as the occasion demands. At close
quarters all kinds of "dirty work" may be
required to finish the job. The great thing about
hand-to-hand fighting is to keep your intelligence
mobile, to seize every opportunity and to be always
prepared to shift your plan of attack with hardly a
second's notice. Every fight differs from every
other fight: no one can do more for you than
suggest possible combinations of circumstances; in
the end it is each man for himself. Practise until
your reactions come like lightning and nothing can
baffle you.

CHAPTER V.

Brighter Training.

IMPROVISED REALISTIC MOBILE TARGET. . . .
IMAGINATIVE PRACTICE IN PASSING FIRE
ORDERS FOR LANDSCAPE TARGET. . . . HOME-
MADE GRENADE RANGE. . . . UNUSUAL FACTS
ABOUT HAND GRENADES. . . . THE RIGHT
WAY TO THROW GRENADES. . . . NEED FOR
THE COMPETITIVE SPIRIT. . . . ANTI-AIRCRAFT
CONCEALMENT.

THE dive bomber is the modern substitute for
artillery, the " tommy " gun is largely taking
the place of the longer-range machine gun, and
streets and houses are supplanting trenches and
dugouts. So far as infantry is concerned, this
means that the range becomes shorter and the
essential speed greater and greater.

In modern warfare targets are seldom stationary,
scarcely ever fully visible, due to the use of smoke
bombs and the clouds rising from burning buildings. Yet much training in shooting is still given
on last war ranges! The rifle is thought by many
only to be a long-range weapon for use at several
hundred yards, whereas to-day it will have to be
brought into play at distances of, say, ten to thirty
yards and against an enemy who will only be

visible for a split second. The chief aim of shooting practice, therefore, should be to teach how to
shoot moving targets at very close range in a
split second.

I have suggested elsewhere various mobile
targets, but I recently had an idea which I believe
will prove useful. Most Home Guards have .22
rifles available and instead of using these on
stationary targets, arrange a practice on the
following lines :—

Choose as terrain a deep quarry or some spot
facing a steep hillside into which shots can be
fired with safety. So long as the hill is really
steep there is no great danger provided sentries are
posted well on the flanks to warn passers-by to
keep away and quiet countryside chosen.

Fix two posts—or use trees if they are available
—about twenty yards apart and about six or seven
feet high. From one to the other stretch a strong
wire, much as a clothes lines is hung. Before at-
taching the second end of the wire, slip over it a
key ring or some similar piece of metal which can
run freely up and down. To this tie the target,
which can be an empty tin or some other suitable
object, but not a stone, as bullets might ricochet.

This has now to be converted from the stationary target into a mobile one. Do this by fixing a
ring, pulley, or something similar to each post
at the top, on the edge facing the firing point. A
long piece of wire is passed through the ring on
top of the left hand post, carried along and passed
through the ring on top of the other post.

If a fifteen yards range is desired—and that is long enough—the long wire will have to be eighty yards. The hanging target is now wired to the middle of the long wire and the two men who operate it are standing approximately thirty yards behind the shooter.

As one man walks or runs away from his post or tree and the other towards it, the target will move at the same speed. The rifleman then fires as many rounds as he can with accuracy or reasonable accuracy, and the test is to see how many hits he can register. It's fun listening for them.

This will provide realistic training which men enjoy far more than the ordinary range practice, and it will prove more helpful in establishing self-confidence should an invasion occur.

For the next three ideas, I am indebted to a Home Guard instructor who kindly mailed them to me :—

Real Practice in Passing on Fire Orders.

Where only three .22 rifles can be obtained, have a dozen men take up the prone position facing a landscape target. No. 1 could be the N.C.O. and Nos. 3, 7 and 11 the riflemen. The N.C.O. gives the order to No. 2, and he passes it along to his neighbour, telling him to wait for the order "Fire," and so on until No. 12 has received it. When No. 12 signals O.K. the order "Fire" is given and the position of the holes in the screen indicate if the instruction has been accurately transmitted.

As a change from the monotony of target practice, set up a number of small wooden blocks or children's bricks and have the volunteer shoot them off the pile one by one, beginning with the uppermost.

If the range is out of doors, have men run at full speed to the firing point, pick up already loaded rifles and shoot without delay or hesitation. This stimulates real service conditions, and competitions with a time limit can be held between squad and squad, adding excitement and interest.

N.C.O.s should think out other variations by way of a change, such as firing from the left shoulder. This is a most useful exercise in preparation for street fighting when it may become essential in firing round corners.

Improvised Grenade Range.

Compulsion has proved necessary for the Home Guard, and I cannot help thinking that it may have been due to dull and boring training. And Home Guard compulsion will fail miserably in its objective unless officers realise that new means of training must continually be devised. Few men, for instance, are sufficiently keen to care about throwing hand grenades for an hour at nothing, as they are frequently expected to do. I admit it is a small point, but if interest is to be retained, interesting targets must be evolved. Even a golfer has a hole for his ball! Remove the hole and the hazards and I prophesy that golf as a game would disappear. It is a psychological fact that a man will not only lose interest in his work if he has nothing to achieve and no competition, but the benefit of the training will largely be lost. I once read a book which alleged that a man batting a ball alone against a wall tires physically in fifteen minutes, while, if he is playing tennis with an opponent, he can continue for hours without undue fatigue.

Instructors should remember this.

To avoid monotony, therefore, hang two ropes from the branch of a tree and tie two other ropes between them to represent a window in a building. Divide the section into two squads, place one on either side of the "window" and see which team can score most direct hits. Direct hits are scored by throwing the dummy hand grenades right through the improvised window.

On another occasion let a cyclist trail a sack of straw behind him—well behind for safety's sake—to represent a passing staff car, and have two teams see how many hits they can register from various ranges.

Such other methods as laying targets on the ground at different distances or digging small trenches as targets should be arranged in order to create competition and interest.

Unusual Facts About Hand Grenades.

In practising with a dummy, the first rule which N.C.O.s must insist upon is that each recruit unscrews the base plug to make sure that the grenade is not primed, in other words, that is is safe to use. If this is not done accidents will arise as sometimes dummies and live grenades get mixed.

The grenade is not thrown in the manner of throwing a stone. It is bowled, as in cricket, but with a higher trajectory, so that in action, the grenade can be dropped over walls, barricades, etc.

The utmost range is about 30 yards, varying with the individual, of course, but in all training, accuracy should be insisted upon, rather than extreme distance.

It is not sufficient to attain proficiency in the standing position, for in war many occasions arise when grenades have to be thrown from the kneeling or prone position. In throwing while kneeling, the knees are kept about one foot apart so that the recruit is in an easy and comfortably-balanced position. This should be frequently practised. If dummies are unobtainable, stones of similar shape and weight (about 1½ lbs.) should be used.

In the prone position the range will be shorter. While throwing, the body rests on the left shoulder, and the pitch is made by bringing the right hand from well behind the body with the same overarm movement. Keep practising this until expert.

When live grenades are used instructors must warn their men of the risk of dropping the grenade after the pin has been removed. What happens is that in the excitement of first experience, or actual war, after the pin has been taken out, while the right hand is drawn back to the throwing position, it hits the parados or back of the trench, knocking the grenade from the recruit's grasp. That is why, in grenade practice with dummies,

trenches should be used to show how easily this
happens. The four seconds between the time the
pin is released and the explosion, allow ample time
for the recruit to pick up the grenade and throw
it clear. Nevertheless, some men seem to panic
and it is therefore essential that when live grenades
are in use an instructor should accompany the
beginner, so that if he drops the bomb, he can
quickly throw it clear.

Another point which should be stressed is that
the moment a live grenade is thrown all present
must obtain protection. In battle this is done by
flinging themselves to the ground and staying flat
till the bits stop flying. This takes several
seconds, and as pieces of shrapnel explode in all
directions, the danger area, especially on hard
ground, is up to a radius of a hundred yards.

In training it must be explained that with proper
care and after sufficient practise with dummies,
the soldier need have no fear of handling or carrying grenades. Each man, on receiving live
grenades, should make sure that the pins are
secure and the levers fit properly into the grooves
provided, before putting them into haversack or
pocket. If the grenade is faulty, he should refuse
to accept it.

The hand grenade is a most demoralising and
useful weapon. It is ideal for clearing machine-
gun nests, trenches, houses and the like, particu-
larly during darkness. In this sort of night fighting, pads should be tied round the boots so that
noise is eliminated. Before entering rooms or
places thought to be in enemy hands, always lob

a grenade in first, but remember to wait till the bits stop flying, before entering. Many a man has lost his life by tossing a grenade into a room and rushing in before the shrapnel has subsided.

After a grenade has been thrown into a room, leap right inside the door with your "tommy" gun or sawn-off shot gun at the "Ready." You must dash right inside, because, doing so, leaves room for your companions to follow you and overwhelm the enemy, or what is left of him.

Men ambushing enemy transport or tank harbours at night must also be freely supplied with grenades. It is a phychological fact that a number of the enemy, being surprised, are more afraid of attackers armed with grenades in addition to rifles and bayonets, than with rifles only.

Another point often overlooked in instruction manuals is that, as a general rule, when a position is " captured," there will be one of the enemy with sufficient courage and initiative to fight back. We have all seen the sort of thing in wild west films; a light is extinguished, a table knocked over or a chair thrown to upset the attackers. This almost invariably happens in the real thing. That is why it is best to destroy the enemy, rather than think of taking prisoners, unless in exceptional circumstances.

If an enemy area is recaptured, the Home Guard must remember to mop up afterwards. This is important, because German soldiers have instructions that when their lines are overrun, as many of them as possible should seek cover in shell holes, dugouts, cellars, attics, etc., so that they can sally forth afterwards, or at night and creatre havoc in the rear.

Anti-Aircraft Concealment

I have seen men in defensive positions lining hedges, waiting for the enemy to attack. These men should, when possible, as we well know, be " inside " the hedge so as to be invisible to hostile aircraft. Not only might the enemy dive-bomb or machine-gun them, but he could probably give their position away to the attackers by the simple means of dropping a message. In some instances cover from the air cannot be obtained by merging into the hedge. Each man, therefore, who has to take up such a position, should make a small "hide" for himself by using his dagger or knife. This is easily and quickly done by cutting a few branches and sticking them into the ground, leaning their tops against the hedge. Partly fill in the gaps between the upper parts of the branches with foliage from the surrounding bushes and a reasonable, personal "hide" is the result.

This has the double advantage of cover from above and from behind, should parachutists be landed suddenly in the rear.

On other occasions, as, for instance, when lining a river bank, the gas cape thrown right over the head and shoulders would be a fairly good anti-aircraft cover. If in the prone position the feet and legs should be curled up when aircraft are overhead.

It is essential that the Home Guard become paratroop and aircraft minded.

CHAPTER VI.

The Superiority of Shot-Guns for Certain Tasks.

How to Identify Enemy at Night. . . .
The Sawn-Off Shot Gun. . . . Firing From
the Hip. . . . Foot Pads.

I BELIEVE the uses of the ordinary shot gun have been overlooked by most Home Guards. A stock of these and of No. 4 shot cartridges, or even heavier—as swan shot—should be kept handy for special jobs. One advantage, of course, is the double barrel, which means that two shots can be fired almost simultaneously.

Shot gun pellets pass through wired windows when hand grenades will not. Indeed, at so near a range as eighteen yards they could probably be used to break the wire netting which Germans put over windows, besides giving the occupants of the room plenty to think about as the lead " pellets " ricochet round and round. These shot guns are available in most districts. It will be noted that I am not recommending them for ordinary street or infantry battles, as the effective

range is not great. But up to fifty yards, fired
at the face, they should put an enemy out of action
without any doubt. In France, in the last war,
they proved useful. Ball ammunition for them is
not, I believe, altogether satisfactory and is in
any cases inferior to the rifle, owing to the shorter
range and poor degree of accuracy.

On dark nights the shot gun, in the right hands,
is superb. What novices must remember is the
great spread of the shot. This should be demon-
strated with, say, No. 4 shot, by firing at forty
yards into a river or lake, so that the future user
will know what a dangerous tool he has. At fifty
yards even such small shot as No. 4 will pass
through a pail, so Heaven help the Nazi who
receives a dose in the face or head. Each cartridge contains about 200 pellets! Another advantage is that the shot gun can put several men out
of action at once. Briefly, for dark night jobs, for
shooting into wired-up windows and for special
tasks, such as making sure that no enemy is lurking
in undergrowth, the shot gun is superior to the
rifle.

For fighting inside buildings and for searching
houses, if no " tommy " gun is available, the
sawn-off shot gun, with No. 4 cartridges, is the
right thing, providing care is taken not to shoot
if the pellets can richochet and hit the shooter or
if the enemy and one's own men are mixed in
fighting. In the latter case the possible spread of
the shot among one's own side would be very
risky. The shot gun should only be used by a
man who is accustomed to it.

Night Identification.

One of the great difficulties at night is that of recognition, more especially if the enemy has infiltrated. On a pitch black night a powerful torch is one of the few possible methods. The disadvantage of this form of challenge is that it gives away the position of your ambush; it must therefore be used with care. On the other hand, the use of a powerful torch is less mad than it appears.

The method of use is to keep quiet and hidden by some form of protection, such as sandbags, until the approaching patrol is within a few feet, or, if possible, passed. Discretion must, of course, be observed: a single man could not fight a hundred, but on the other hand he could probably take on several opponents if he were armed with a shot gun or " tommy " gun. And, naturally, the position is altered again if he is one of a number.

In the right use of a torch the advantage is with the user. A lone sniper using one can hold it alongside the barrel of his rifle with the left hand, waiting till the possible target is within range of the beam. He then switches it on, identifies his enemy as such, shoots fast, switches off and " scrams." But the torch must be a powerful one.

Some riflemen consider it best to strap the torch to the barrel. I prefer to hold it in the palm of the left hand, using the fingers to grip the barrel as well as possible. True, owing to the insecure grip, the recoil of the shot will upset the aim, but as the range is point blank, this is quite unimportant.

All Home Guards should obtain range practise in this sort of night work, using their Service rifles.

If there are several Home Guards together, one holds and operates the torch for identification to enable the others to aim. He holds it at arm's length in case of retaliation, so that he is unlikely to be hit. The Home Guards must be quick on the trigger, and the shooting is easy, as the range will be less than twenty yards. The moment the enemy has collected his wits, out goes the torch and off go the Home Guards—that is, if they are still outnumbered. But the torch must be extinguished the moment *before* the enemy begins shooting. He will have been dazzled by the glare and his aim will inevitably be wild—but it may be lucky. Remember the initiative is with the torch bearer, who is shooting from behind protection.

For all night work boots with rubber soles should be donned, or else pads should be tied round the Service issue to make their use silent. The Japanese have been employing the latter method with effect.

Firing From the Hip·

All soldiers should obtain practise in shooting from the hip while charging a target. In this method, only employed when there is not time to mount the rifle to the shoulder, the eye is focussed on the target and the rifle will, instinctively, point towards it. Firing from the hip will often be necessary in the event of invasion. The range must, of course, be short, otherwise there cannot be accuracy. A man should easily be able to hit a newspaper at 25 yards, and one can be propped up and used as a target against a safe background of steep hillside. At the moment of firing, the rifle must be very tightly held with both hands to " take " the recoil. Part of the recoil is also "taken" by the right forearm, and the butt itself is tucked well into the side of the hip. On no account must the beginner fire from the stomach, otherwise the recoil may prove not only painful, but dangerous. Men cannot be expected to acquit themselves in battle unless they have had this sort of realistic practise with their own rifles.

D

CHAPTER VII.

I Caught a Traitor, But!

TRUTH is stranger than fiction. If what I am about to relate had not happened to me personally, I should not have believed that such things were possible in England. During the early days of the bombing of London, I had a civil job helping Sir William Goode at the Ministry of Food. I mention this because the nature of our work, which dealt with communications, meant that one had to be prepared to be on duty at all hours of the day and night. On this occasion, I had been on an evening shift and had arranged to meet my wife and go to the country on a train leaving London at 10.15. Having been on duty for approximately sixteen hours, I was extremely tired.

It happened to be a Sunday, so there were not many people travelling. My wife and I entered the compartment and took corner seats facing one another. A few minutes later a man got in and occupied one of the vacant corners. I took little notice of him beyond just registering the fact that he was very thin and pale and wore neither hat, nor collar. Shortly before the train left a young and attractive woman took the last corner; she got out her knitting and settled to work. Although the guns were blazing away and the Luftwaffe hovering noisily overhead, I was so tired that I gradually dozed off, leaving my wife to read in the dim light provided.

After we had gone some distance I was awakened by a touch on the foot from my wife. Holding her Sunday paper between herself and the man in the other corner, she tried to indicate something to me by holding out her hand with the fingers spread wide. I could not make out what she meant, but she explained to me later on that she wanted me to appreciate that she believed we had a Fifth Columnist in the carriage.

I gathered that something was wrong, but could not guess the answer until my wife handed me a slip of paper on which she had scribbled, " I have been watching that man and he seems agitated. All the way down he has chain smoked and referred to something in a notebook and looked at his watch and out of the window, even though it is dark. I think he is a spy."

My first reaction—probably the normal one of every Britisher—was to say, " Impossible; things like that don't happen in this country." But my wife is not given to scare-mongering. I began to gather my wits together after my doze and on taking in the situation it certainly appeared that our companion was strangely intent on something.

Just at this moment the train began to slow down and he rose and opened the window. Obviously he was going to get out. " Ah," I thought, " this is his station and he's probably scared of the Nazi 'planes," for we could still hear them buzzing about. In my own mind, by this time, I had classed him as a railway lines-man or something of that kind, basing my judg-ment on his general appearance and dress.

The train was just running into the station when the action started like lightning. I realised suddenly that the fellow had opened the window on the far side—the one away from the platform. Before one could say "knife," he had stretched his arm out at full length and was waving a power-ful torch. A moment later he had opened the compartment door, and I thought he was going to fall out on to the line. Instinctively I shouted, " That's the wrong side!" and he replied in a tone and accent which practically proved him an Englishman, " Thanks, I didn't notice." As he spoke, he swung round, dashed past us, swung the other door open and jumped out.

I was not in H.G. uniform or I would probably have seized him, but through my sleepy brain ran the thought that I couldn't arrest anyone while I was in civilian clothes, that there would be the most awful fuss if I attempted to interfere and that perhaps he was, after all, a railway employee who was dangerously but not treacherously signal-ling to a comrade.

Then I looked out of the window and saw him vanishing into the night at the double. I suddenly came to my full senses and knew that it was a case of now or never. Shouting to my wife to "tell the guard to hold up the train," I leapt from the compartment and dashed after the man.

As he came to the ticket collector he said " Evening," and ran up the steps. By this time I was functioning normally again, and I thought that he was probably a local man and therefore traceable. Hurrying up to the ticket collector myself, I said, " I see you know that man. I was after him because he was flashing a torch in the black-out, but I suppose he is all right?" To my surprise, the porter replied, " No, I don't think I've ever seen him before."

So once again I gave chase at full speed. The man heard my footsteps, turned, and came back towards me. " Were you running after me?" he asked with complete coolness.

" I certainly was," I replied. " Why did you flash that light out of the carriage window?"

His answer was prompt enough. " You were right to chase me. I might have been anyone, but, as a matter of fact, I am on secret work, co-operating with the police."

" Oh," I said. " What police?"

" Come over here," he said, drawing me under a partially blacked-out station lamp. " Here are my credentials." He then showed me a card with his photograph pasted on it and printed Scotland Yard, Metropolitan Police Branch," with other details which were in too small type for me to read. It certainly looked as if I had made a bad mistake, so I apologised, and in a moment he was off. On my way back to the train, I reflected that the whole business sounded thoroughly odd and unsatisfactory—but what more could I do?

Back in the compartment—for the guard had responded to my wife's appeal and had held the train the necessary moment—I told my wife that the whole story sounded distinctly fishy, and she heartily agreed. The sensation had broken the ice round the other woman and she concurred with my wife's account of the man's peculiar behaviour, which had apparently been worrying her also.

We were only a few minutes from our destination and I decided to ring up Scotland Yard and ask them if they had a man stationed at that particular spot. I was already beginning to feel that I should have hung on to the suspect when our travelling companion confirmed my opinion by remarking that the station at which he had got out was adjacent to one of the most important military objectives in the county.

I told the story to the Yard within a few minutes. The officer to whom I spoke was quite definite in his reply. " We have no man operating in the vicinity you mention. In any case none of our men would do what this fellow did. He is obviously a Fifth Columnist. As it is very late I will take the matter up myself and get men put on to the job."

I thanked him and made him promise to let me know what happened, but I am sorry to say I have never had a word from Scotland Yard.

Now, perhaps, I flatter myself, but I believe I did as well as the majority of Home Guards would have done in the circumstances—perhaps a little better, for I did at least try and get the man, but the terrible fact remains that I had actually got my hands on a traitor and I let him go.

I would not make such an error a second time, and I hope that other Home Guards would not make it once. And it must be remembered that this all happened in the early days of the Home Guard, the days when few of us were on our toes. In another chapter I shall deal with the vital lessons which are to be learned from this failure, but for the moment I want to complete the task which I have set myself of proving to you that there are Fifth Columnists in this country.

I am not asking anyone to believe the amazing rumours and spy stories which come round through the charlady's daughter's husband's sister-in-law, but I am going to relate facts which have happened to me personally and for which I can vouch.

About a year before the war I was working in connection with a literary agency, and in the course of business I was asked to call on a certain woman who lived near Notting Hill Gate. At the present moment I admit I do not remember either her name or her actual address; I was meeting a great number of comparative strangers, and I did not trouble to remember all of them.

I arrived at this woman's house and found her to be a middle-aged spinster of a somewhat masculine type, though not aggressively so. I have met many actual German Nazis of the most fanatical type, but never have I met anyone to whom Hitler and the Nazi creed had been more

perfectly " sold " than this woman. Her room
was littered with pictures and photographs of
Hitler, and though war had not broken out, she
regarded him as the coming Saviour of the world.
She had read "Mein Kampf," but that seemed
only to have increased her fervent adoration. I
suspected her of mental unbalance, a suspicion
which was strengthened when she showed me one
of Hitler's photographs and exclaimed, " Look at
the power in his face . . . look at his eyes . . even
if this man asked me to sleep with him I should
not be able to resist."

I do not say that this type is a common one, but
where one exists, others will develop. My guess
is that to-day that woman is pretending to be
wholeheartedly working for the Allied cause,
while her infatuation for Hitler is such that if she
is not already acting as a Fifth Columnist, the
Nazis would certainly find her a ready assistant
should they succeed in invading the country.

One another occasion, also shortly before the
war, I met a German Jew in a London hotel.
For some reason we got into a conversation which
lasted well into the night. Bear in mind that this
episode and the one in Notting Hill Gate both
occurred before the war and before either of my
companions knew for certain that there would be a
war, so that what they said should be taken as
quite unprejudiced. With regard to this Jew, the
interesting thing was that he was a widely
travelled, fine type of man, who had fled from
Nazi persecution some months previously. He
hated the Nazis and their ways with a loathing

which cannot be described in words, but which could be heard in every tone of his voice and seen in every expression of his mobile features. Inevitably the conversation turned on the possibility of war between Germany and Great Britain. Neither of us thought that hostilities would actually materialise.

The latter part of our talk stands vividly in my memory.

I decided to put a direct question to him and said, " Suppose that war comes and with it a German invasion of this country? I presume you will fight with us as you so hate the Nazis?"

" Oh, no," he replied. " You don't understand. I would be on the side of the invaders. Germany is ' home ' to me, as Scotland is to you." He paused a moment. " Look at it this way," he continued. " While, of course, it could not happen, if England were to invade Scotland, on which side would you fight, even though you had lived in England for years and were convinced that her cause was right?" I had to confess that I would fight with the Scots, right or wrong. What Scotsman wouldn't?

Presumably this man is at large, for he is about the last type of alien who would be interned. Yet, if invasion takes place, he would be an enemy within our gates. There must be others like him.

I am the last person to advocate wholesale internment at the present moment, but I do say that all aliens should be carefully supervised and the moment invasion occurs every one of them should be rounded up and immediately segregated. Probably the authorities already plan to do this—but who knows?

After writing the above I chanced upon the following review in the *Sunday Times* for February 8th, which I am taking the liberty of quoting because it reinforces my conviction of our danger in an extraordinary way.*

> " It (the book) is also valuable as a first-hand account of the treatment of the French authorities since the beginning of the war of the anti-Nazi refugees. Herr Lania spent the first four months of the war in an internment camp, where conditions were bad, though certainly not Dauchau-like. But though he personally suffered, Herr Lania does not minimise the extent of the problem with which the French would have been faced had they seriously attempted to sort out the good and the bad refugees. As the German troops were approaching the internment camp, he says, a strange thing happened :
> ' From one day to the next all masks fell. Several of the Germans, a few of the Austrians openely expressed their sympathy with the Nazis. ' Just wait in a few days you'll be studying camp life in Dachau,' they shouted at me and Walter.' "

One other instance seems worth recording since it happened to a man whose word I know can be relied on implicitly—Mr. Leonard H. Woodford, the Managing Director of the firm of publishres who have issued this book.

One early morning, about 2 a.m., a very loud knocking at the door awakened Mr. Woodford, and he sleepily got up to find an officer in British uniform on his threshold. Speaking brusquely and impatiently, the officer demanded to be informed the way to a certain point, intimating that

* *The Darkest Hour*, by Leo Lania. Gollancz, Ltd., 8s. 6d. Reviewed by Alexander Werth.

he was in charge of a convoy and had lost his
way. His manner, having given rise to suspicions,
Mr. Woodford gave him only very brief directions and went back to bed. Not until he was
thinking over the matter did it occur to him
how completely improbable it all was. No British
officer would have knocked up a stranger like that
in the small hours; he would have telephoned to
the police or to the local Home Guard for his
directions, since he would have known that the
latter is on duty all night. Moreover, no British
officer would have been so discourteous, and, still
further, there was no convoy in sight. Unfortu-
nately, it was too late to do much by the time
Mr. Woodford realised that he had been the victim
of a Fifth Columnist; he rang up the local police
station, but got no reply, so he telephoned to
another branch, who expressed gratitude for the
information and proposed to have an immediate
search made for the disguised officer.

It would appear conclusive that there are Fifth
Columnists in our midst. I firmly believe that
they are comparatively few, probably not more
than a few thousand in the whole country, and
most of them will never appear in their true colours
unless we are actually invaded. We need not
panic over the position, but we do need to be
materially and mentally prepared.

Many statements have been issued, some by
people who ought to know better, to the effect that
there are no Fifth Columnists in this country.
The purpose of this chapter is to prove from
personal experience that there are certainly a few.

The casualness with which the matter is treated is more than alarming. I know one branch of our War departments where the scantiest attention is paid to passes, and I suggested to a very high-up military man that a brisk good morning and a wave of a pocket book should not suffice as a free entrance and the run of the place. His reply was interesting. " I raised the matter at a meeting," he said, " and I was laughed at and labelled a funk." The recent "capture" of the B.B.C. during Home Guard exercises and other experiences of a like kind do suggest that a stricter attention should be maintained.

I admit that at the present time when raids are few, the risk may be infinitesimal, but at the time of my conversation raids were nightly and parachutists expected momentarily in that area. In war it must never be assumed that there are no traitors. There are always traitors—termed in these days Fifth Columnists; there always have been and there always will be. There are also always men and *women*, who, because of the yellowness of their hearts, will become Quislings through a combination of fear and admiration for the enemy who occupy their particular area. Remember these points.

CHAPTER VIII.

Treatment for Fifth Columnists.

I MAKE no apology in urging all Home Guards to be at all times on their toes and to watch for spies, with special attentiveness during periods of heavy bombing or of threatened invasion. They should be too wide awake to be taken in by any clever ruse. My publisher and I both confess frankly that in our separate ways we acted like mugs. In excuse, we can only plead that we behaved as most Britishers would have done in like circumstances, and we, at any rate, have learnt our lesson.

After all, the majority of us, as honest, law-abiding citizens, are totally inexperienced in such matters, whereas such people as the Germans have been trained for the purpose for years.

First of all, let us consider the grave blunders that I myself made in regard to the enemy in the train.

The fact that I was in " civvies " makes no difference; in no case was I fighting, but merely arresting a fifth columnist, who was himself not in uniform. Secondly, the fellow's story was not

63

water-tight and sounded suspicious. I should have been wide awake enough to see this and to have detained him, by force, if necessary. · Had he been innocent, in all the circumstances he could not have objected to my taking him for examination to the local Home Guard commander or to the nearest police station.

While speaking about the police, I should like to say that in country districts I consider it much more safe to escort a man or pass on any information to the Home Guard, first, then to the Army, and, last of all, to the police. This is not to say that I do not appreciate the police, but the average country constable is not war-minded or alert. Probably most of us remember when Mr. Eden first called for volunteers for the Home Guard. In my own district the police lost the names and addresses of many of those who offered their services, my own included, which suggests that they were not very efficient!

In this spy case, if I had taken the suspect to the local Home Guard H.Q. authority they would have communicated with Scotland Yard at once and we should have ended by capturing a Fifth Columnist, instead of letting one go.

The moment a Fifth Columnist has been certainly spotted, the entire Home Guard and police force of the district should be called out and a cordon thrown round the whole area, which should not be released until he has been captured. If he has been seen in a coastal area, the Naval authorities and R.A.F. Coastal Command would also be warned, as he might try to escape by

means of a small boat. If inland and he is anywhere near an aerodrome, then the R.A.F. should
also be advised.

I stress these points because I myself know of
at least one case in which the requisite action was
not taken with sufficient promptitude. Time is
the essence of the business. Get your cordon out
before the suspect has a chance to slip through.

The error my publisher made was in opening
his door. During a "blitz" the man who knocked
might well have been a fanatical parachutist, and
Mr. Woodford might easily have been killed as
soon as he exposed himself. When a knock came
at such a late hour, he should have answered it
first of all by shouting from the side of the door,
well behind the wall for protection.

When you look into it, the whole thing resolves
itself into the fact that we are an unusupicious
nation and entirely unused to spies and war on
our doorstep.

If proof is needed that spies and traitors can
remain among their friends and neighbours quite
unsuspected for years, the answer can be seen in
the recent outbreak of sabotage in South Africa.
Here large numbers of enemy agents were arrested
after doing considerable damage to factories and
telephone communications.

I do not say that we have a large percentage
of traitors in this country, but I am positive that
in certain circumtances, such as invasion, we
should find several thousand enemies within the
gates. Nor are these the beautiful women spies

E

of fiction or even the Mata Haris of real life: they are just ordinary looking men and women.

Have we not all been warned that " Careless Talk Costs Lives "?   In this case it would seem that the authorities think as I do!

Personally, I would go so far as to say that what might be termed the " best " enemy agents will be found in one or other of our uniforms. Where you have hundreds of thousands of men as, for instance, in the Army and the Home Guard, it would be impossible for those in command to be satisfied of the individual loyalty of each.

A spy's whole training is based on knowing how to avoid being suspected.   Traitors in our midst would no doubt cover themselves with a cloak of great and obvious loyalty, being among the keenest and hardest workers for the country, until such time came as they would be useful to the enemy.   Not all spies speak with a broken accent or dress up as nurses or nuns : such disguises are too obvious, and, in my point of view, most unlikely, in spite of all the dramatic reports. Spying is not glorified amateur theatricals: the most successful traitor is he who best hides the fact, and it is our business to be always on the alert.

Watch Out for These.

It is out of the question to provide a complete list of all the things a Fifth Columnist might do, but the following methods have been, or might easily be, used.

A recent issue of the *Readers' Digest* reprinted from *Life* an article by A. Polyakov, in which he recounted how Fifth Columnists in Russia indicated Russian positions to the Nazi aircraft by furrows ploughed in a field converging to point to different targets.

In a case in which I personally assisted, two men, one carrying a suitcase, turned out to be Fifth Columnists. I don't think they were actually caught, but some of the wire which they had been using was found on a common. It was insulated wire which an expert assured me could have been used to signal by wireless to nearby aircraft. This happened within a hundred miles of London and near a military target.

Other methods which may be expected will be chalk marks and code messages and possibly clothes lines pointing in the direction of objectives. Incoming messages to Headquarters ought also to be very carefully checked up, as undoubtedly spies will employ this technique to disorganise or ruin plans. One way of checking incoming calls is to check up in the telephone directory the number from which the call is supposed to have been made and then ring back and verify it. In many cases, of course, messages are automatically confirmed by the recipients recognising the voice of the sender.

Unless runners are known, it is always a sound idea to make them sign their names and compare these signatures with those of their identity cards. If there is anything suspicious about the business, hold the man for further identification.

There are a variety of commonsense ways of checking up, such as by asking the runner for the name of his C.O. and ringing up the local H.Q. to make sure that the man is a member of that unit. But be careful to guard against a trick once played on me. The man told me to check him up by telephoning a certain number and asking for another man called Walker. I did this and was fully reassured as to my man's credentials. I was young then, it is true, but then some of our Home Guard are young in experience. I ought not to have accepted that challenge, because some one had been "planted" at the end of that telephone line with the correct answers, and, like a fool, I fell for it.

Spies and traitors, or, for that matter, ordinary enemy scouts, will undoubtedly employ light signals and perhaps torches to convey messages to aircraft and to their own trooops. Flat roofs, upper windows, trees, skylights and so on should be carefully watched for this kind of thing.

I make no apology for having dealt with what may strike some readers as elementary stuff, but rest assured that spies and traitors are wily folk and take some catching. More especially must the Englishman guard against his instinctive kindness and trustingness in time of war. The enemy will stop at nothing. He will use local men and women as Fifth Columnists where he can, and, while we should like to believe that he would never find any one willing to do his dirty work, we cannot dismiss the possibility. Remember, bribes and threats will be employed—even, perhaps, threats of murdering children.

I am confident that Britain is free from traitors to a greater extent than any other country in the world, but that does not mean that she is utterly exempt.

Bird In Hand.

I have spoken of the need for care in not allowing oneself to be fooled. But it ought to be made clear to all volunteers that being on sentry duty does not mean that one should shoot anyone on the least suspicion. I mention this because at a lecture I recently attended the speaker said, " When in doubt—shoot." This is obviously a most dangerous doctrine. There are partially deaf and blind people and there is no need to let the trigger off too soon. If we were actually being invaded, it would be a different matter. Frequently we hear of some suspicious, but possibly innocent, wayfarer being killed by an over-enthusiastic sentry. I would be willing to bet that not one of these people has been, in reality, a spy or a traitor.

Anyone who does not respond to a challenge should be kept covered and the matter investigated. The sentry can either approach with rifle levelled or fire a warning shot just in advance of the individual. Of course, in certain circumstances, instructions to shoot at sight must be given, but ordinarily the greatest discretion should be used.

That does not mean that there should be any carelessness. In a paper the other day I saw a photograph of a sentry holding up a car which his colleague was examining. The sentry, with fixed bayonet, stood about three yards on one side, while immediately on the other side of the driver his companion was examining credentials.   I forget the exact caption to the picture, but it was to the effect that "no inefficiency at this factory." N.C.O.s should stage a similar example and have their men spot what was wrong.

As the reader may have seen, the position of the driver immediately between the two sentries was incorrect.   Had he started to be obstructive, the armed sentry would have been unable to deal with him without killing or badly wounding his comrade.   In the circumstances, all the driver need have done was to swing round, whip out a revolver and shoot the armed sentry and then dispose of the unarmed one.   The armed sentry ought to have watched his stance.

The rule is that the armed sentry should always stand behind the man who is being vetted, so that the suspect cannot observe his actions.   He must choose his position so that he can shoot instantaneously without any risk of his bullet passing through the suspect and killing the second sentry.

When searching a prisoner for weapons, always stand behind him and not in front, so that he cannot employ the crutch kick.

A good test for Home Guard is to have someone arrive suddenly by arrangement and then ask a volunteer to step forward and carry out an investigation as though the man were an enemy suspect. It will be interesting to see how this is done. Possibly the sentry will command " Hands up " and then ask for the identity card.   The man should be advised to produce it quickly and walk up to the sentry with it.   As the sentry takes it,

it is highly probable that he will uncover the man
with his rifle; in this case the suspect should grab
the rifle and twist it into his own hands. This
is an excellent example of what a sentry should
not do.

Next an experienced Home Guard should
demonstrate how the job ought to be done. The
suspect should be ordered to turn round and place
both hands on the top of his head while he is
questioned. In the meantime, the sentry keeps
him covered and is never less than five yards away.
The suspect should then be ordered not to turn
round on pain of being shot, but to turn out the
contents of his pockets on to the ground, leaving
the linings of the pockets hanging out. Still with
his back to the sentry, he should be ordered to
move ten yards away while the contents of the
pockets are checked up. All this time the man
must be covered with—in actual war—a loaded
rifle, with a round in the chamber, and fixed
bayonet, and he must rest both hands on top of
his head. If there are two sentries, the matter
is simplified, but the principle is the same.

Should a soldier have to guard several prisoners,
he should order them to stand ten yards off—so
that he cannot be rushed—with their hands resting
on their helmets. If possible, a better proceeding
is to tie them up.

Another bit of useful knowledge is to know how
to tie up a man. It is almost impossible to tie
a man securely if he is to be left alone, as he will
usually manage to wriggle over to some wall and
rasp through his ropes against the edge of it.

Therefore, if a prisoner has to be left, his tying up is no easy matter. It is difficult to hit the happy medium of avoiding so tight a tying that the circulation is stopped and so loose a one that he is able to cut it through. Occasions occur when a man has to be secured with rope. The best method then is to tie the hands and feet tightly together. Then, laying the prisoner on his face, pull back his feet and tie them to his hands, then pass a rope through the arms and legs and up round his throat, so that if he struggles he will choke himself.

Practise this with due caution as part of training.

Should you yourself be taken prisoner, the best chance of escape is to "play dumb," as the expression goes. Let the enemy think you are as meek and mild as a dove and are really rather thankful to be captured. Be friendly with the man who is guarding you. Play no tricks at all and obey every order, while watching your opportunity. No one can tell how or when a chance of escape will arise.

You may be taken into a room with electric light and be able to put it out at a suitable moment and make your escape in the dark.

The whole secret is to keep quiet until the sentry is tired and unsuspecting and then to act suddenly. Various unarmed combat methods outlined in the *Home Guard Encyclopædia* might be adopted. Escape is not easy, but is often possible.

I have said nothing as to how traitors who may be captured should be treated. It is said that in actual warfare the only right thing to do is to leave the body in the middle of the local High Street with a notice attached, " This was a traitor to Britain," as an example to anyone who might be tempted to emulate him.   If circumstances permit, the best thing is to leave the decision to the C.O. Provided it is certain that the person in question is a Fifth Columnist, something very drastic must indubitably be done.   Whatever we do we must be tough minded enough, and ruthless enough, not to allow the suspect to slip through our fingers. In brief, we must be prepared to treat 'em rough.

Possibly, even before this book is on sale, this country will experience an airborne landing. Purely for political reasons, in my view, Hitler and Co. must reply to our " Commandos," even if only on a small scale.

CHAPTER IX.

The Right Way to Lecture.

GETTING YOUR MESSAGE OVER. . . .
CONCENTRATING ON ESSENTIALS.

THE normal comment to many of the lectures given to the Home Guard is that they are dry and unhelpful. What is the reason for this? Probably it is because the men who are selected to lecture have, in most cases, received no training in the technique of teaching and imparting knowledge and do not know how to " get their stuff across." In civil life the majority of N.C.O.s get no chance of speaking to an audience, and a few words may therefore be useful.

Most lecturers are far too verbose. The essence of the message is lost in repetitive phrases. Actual repetition of facts again is a very common fault. Lecturers will go on hammering a point home until the students are sick of it.

Lecturers should therefore keep these points in the forefront of their minds: speak concisely and cut out repetition.

But those two points are not in themselves sufficient to grip an audience.

Anyone who lectures on a subject must be a master of it. And if he really knows what he is

75

talking about, he will almost certainly be interesting, provided he takes a little care in his theme.

Secondly, a lecturer should put himself, as far as possible in the place of his hearers. If he uses a little thought and imagination, he will realise, for instance, that a lecture cannot be helpful if it contains nothing but material already given to the Home Guard by other instructors. Again, by putting himself in the place of his audience, he will be able to remember all the things which a man ignorant of the subject would like to know.

A lecturer should not only read up his subject and have had practical experience of it, but he should find time beforehand to sit down quietly and think it over so that he can find new ideas, inferences and illustrations. It is the new, useful and original material in a lecture that sticks in the minds of the hearers.

This question of illustrations is a very important one. As far as possible find out the type of men to whom you will be lecturing and the kind of life they lead and draw your illustrations from objects which are reasonably familiar. I remember at one time attending a series of lectures on a somewhat abstruse subject; the lecturer, who was a wireless expert and salesman, illustrated all his points by wireless allusions, induction coils, positive and negatives, leads, and so on, which were entirely meaningless to me. No one in the audience should have to ask the lecturer to explain his illustrations; they are intended to be the explanation. To take an extreme case to-day, it is no good illustrating a lecture by taking electric light as a simile if you are talking to a handful of men from a village where only candles are used!

To prove that hard thinking and real knowledge are required, let me quote two examples of the sort of thing which happens.

Number one is an N.C.O. whom we may picture as a conventional sort of fellow, well read in his own subject, but without the imagination to put himself in the place of his hearers. He gives a talk on a subject with the general and boring title of "Musketry"—the sort of uninspired title such a man would select.

He then proceeds to tell his class the technical names of all parts of the rifle, without any attempt to dramatise them : " This is the foresight and this is the swivel . . ." and so on, part after part. Then he instructs in the same monotonous fashion, " It should be remembered in cleaning the rifle that the sling be removed . . ." quoting or paraphrasing from the text book, but without any individuality of presentment. Then he explains the mechanism of the rifle and shows how it is held. Meticulously he gives details of the first and second trigger pressures, how many seconds it should take for the soldier to aim and shoot, and so forth.

In other words, he rambles on with a lot of elementary repetition which every man issued with a rifle should have learnt long before. Probably every one of them has learnt them by heart, and it will hardly be surprising that that lecturer will complain afterwards that the class did not show much interest or enthusiasm.

Number 2 is an N.C.O., who has got some idea of practical work and knows that his class wants to get down to real possibilities. He knows, too, that they have reached a certain standard in training. He opens up much more on these lines : " I am going to talk to-night on ' Close Range Shooting in Battle.' I shall skip all the things which you ought to know, and I assume you do know, and get down to points which are usually neglected in training. You are to remember that what I say now follows on what you have already been taught.

" In the heat of the fight a man will often drop his cartridge in the mud. Remember that in this case you must wipe it clean before inserting it, or you run a grave risk of having it jam in the chamber. This is where jamming usually occurs and therefore every care must be taken to keep the chamber perfectly clean.

" In battle you may find that you have fired three rounds at the enemy. The moment you get an opportunity, fill up the magazine, as by doing so you have five chances of saving your life instead of two.

" In street fighting, in woods and such places, there is no time for the elaborate aiming which you have been taught on the range. Owing to smoke and to the movement of the enemy, you will often have to employ snap shooting. For this reason use every effort to get practise at mobile targets by devising a range such as the one described in this book."

This indicates the right sort of material to give the troops. They are usually keen enough to learn, but they need something to get their teeth into.

In all lectures the speaker should use every opportunity to bring out the need for ferocity and fierceness—wherever possible he ought to do all he can to inspire in his hearers the fighting spirit—it is this savage determination to conquer or die which is so utterly necessary in the individual soldier.

All lecturers vary in their methods; some like to write out a lecture in full and deliver it with frequent references to their papers; others prefer full notes, which they can elaborate; and others again, usually those with considerable experience, can lecture without notes at all. But, as a general rule, it is wise to jot down the main headings and to construct a talk with a beginning, a middle and end. Then, if it should be necessary to deviate from the plan, it will be simple to come back to the straight and narrow way without fear of missing an important point. The peroration, or conclusion, should be a brisk, decisive summing up of the chief points dealt with, but care must be taken not to make this a mere repetition in little. The lecturer should, if possible, use actual illustrations from experiences of his own; the human mind retains a " story," which appeals to the imagination better than a series of facts.

The importance of question time cannot be too strongly emphasised. This is the period when difficulties are smoothed out, points that may have been slurred are brought forward, contingencies are discussed. All soldiers should be encouraged to take the initiative at question time and the lecturer should be sure enough of his subject to discuss questions and not merely answer them by the words of the book. After all, there are often several points of view on one illustration of tactics.

Question time, moreover, is the time when the lecturer can assess the mentality of the individuals in his class. Nothing will demonstrate more clearly the slow thinking, but sure brain, the quick, showy type that acts well in an emergency but cannot plan far ahead; the stolid backbone type that will never get anywhere much on his own initiative, but can be trusted to obey orders till death.

A lecturer may often find it difficult to collect sufficient material to fill the allotted lecture period. In that case, cut the lecture short and lengthen the questions and discussion. Make it an informal and round-table affair. Don't bore the class by dragging out a quarter of an hour's work to fill twenty-five minutes; you will only have the class ragged and inattentive and ill-disposed to ask intelligent questions.

Before leaving this lecture subject, I should like to add that owing to red tape, all over the country valuable time is being wasted in the reading out of endless notices and data sent to the N.C.O.s. Notices should be carefully sorted and only those read that are applicable to the unit. By judicious selection and the wise use of a notice board hours of training time can be saved during a year.

Made and Printed in Great Britain by the Lewes Press (Wightman & Co., Ltd.), Friars Walk, Lewes, Sussex.

Lightning Source UK Ltd.
Milton Keynes UK
UKOW06f1351270916

283933UK00008B/141/P